10/12

P9-EAO-965

Pebble Plus

Living in a Biome

Life in a Rain Forest

by Carol K. Lindeen

Consulting Editor: Gail Saunders-Smith, Ph.D.

Consultant: Sandra Mather, Professor Emerita
Department of Geology and Astronomy, West Chester University
West Chester, Pennsylvania

Capstone
press

Mankato, Minnesota

Pebble Plus is published by Capstone Press
151 Good Counsel Drive, P.O. Box 669, Mankato, Minnesota 56002
http://www.capstonepress.com

1 2 3 4 5 6 08 07 06 05 04 03

Library of Congress Cataloging-in-Publication Data
Lindeen, Carol K., 1976–
     Life in a rain forest / by Carol K. Lindeen.
     p. cm.—(Pebble plus: Living in a biome)
     Summary: Simple text and photographs introduce the rain forest biome,
including the environment, plants, and animals.
     Includes bibliographical references (p. 23) and index.
     ISBN 0-7368-3403-6 (softcover) ISBN 0-7368-2102-3 (hardcover)
     1. Rain forest animals—Juvenile literature. 2. Rain forest plants—Juvenile literature.
[1. Rain forest animals. 2. Rain forest plants.] I. Title.
QH86.L57 2004
578.734—dc21   2002155685

Editorial Credits
Martha E. H. Rustad, editor; Kia Adams, designer and illustrator; Juliette Peters, cover production designer; Kelly Garvin, photo researcher;
     Eric Kudalis, product planning editor

Photo Credits
Ann & Rob Simpson, 4–5
Corbis/Galen Rowell, cover
Digital Vision, 1, 10–11
Eda Rogers, 6–7
James P. Rowan, 8–9, 18–19
Minden Pictures/Frans Lanting, 12–13, 20–21
Tom Stack & Associates/Inga Spence, 14–15
Visuals Unlimited/Inga Spence, 16–17

Note to Parents and Teachers

The Living in a Biome series supports national science standards related to life science. This book describes and illustrates animal and plant life in rain forests. The photographs support early readers in understanding the text. This book also introduces early readers to subject-specific vocabulary words, which are defined in the Glossary section. Early readers may need assistance to read some words and to use the Table of Contents, Glossary, Read More, Internet Sites, and Index/Word List sections of the book.

Word Count: 146
Early-Intervention Level: 13

Table of Contents

What Are Rain Forests?

A rain forest is a large area of land covered with trees and plants. Rain falls almost every day in a rain forest.

Rain forests grow near the equator. They also grow along some sea coasts.

Rain Forests

Rain Forest Animals

Snakes hunt in rain forest trees. They also slither across the rain forest floor.

Tree frogs hop onto tree branches. They eat insects. Many tree frogs are bright colors.

Apes swing from vines high
in the rain forest canopy.

Rain Forest Plants

Tall trees keep the rain
from soaking into the ground.
The tops of tall trees form
the rain forest canopy.

Figs grow on fig trees
in rain forests. Birds
and monkeys eat figs.

17

Ferns grow on the forest floor in the canopy's shade. Ferns have many narrow leaves.

Living Together

Rain forest animals live in the trees or on the ground. Many plants grow in rain forests. Rain forests are full of life.

Glossary

canopy—the layer of treetops formed by the tallest trees in the rain forest; most rain forest animals live in the canopy.

coast—land next to an ocean or sea

equator—the imaginary line around the middle of Earth; the equator is halfway between the North Pole and the South Pole; some places near the equator are very hot.

fig—a small, sweet fruit with tiny seeds

forest floor—the lowest area of a rain forest; little sunlight reaches the forest floor.

insect—a small animal with a hard outer shell, six legs, three body sections, and two antennas; most insects have two or four wings.

soak—to make something very wet

vine—a plant with a long stem that climbs up trees and other plants; vines also grow along the ground.

Read More

Gray, Shirley W. *Rain Forests.* First Reports. Minneapolis: Compass Point Books, 2001.

Richardson, Adele D. *Rain Forests.* The Bridgestone Science Library. Mankato, Minn.: Bridgestone Books, 2001.

Trumbauer, Lisa. *What Are Forests?* Earth Features. Mankato, Minn.: Pebble Books, 2002.

Internet Sites

Do you want to find out more about rain forests?
Let FactHound, our fact-finding hound dog, do the research for you.

Here's how:

1) Visit *http://www.facthound.com*

2) Type in the **Book ID** number: **0736821023**

3) Click on **FETCH IT**.

FactHound will fetch Internet sites picked by our editors just for you!

Index/Word List